FIGHT SONGS

FIGHT SONGS

CAL FREEMAN

 EYEWEAR PUBLISHING

First published in 2017
by Eyewear Publishing Ltd
Suite 333, 19-21 Crawford Street
Marylebone, London w1h 1pj
United Kingdom

Cover design and typeset by Edwin Smet
Cover photograph by Eric Patrick Kelly
Printed in England by TJ International Ltd, Padstow, Cornwall

isbn 978-1-911335-65-8

*Eyewear wishes to thank Jonathan Wonham for his
generous patronage of our press.*

WWW.EYEWEARPUBLISHING.COM

CAL FREEMAN

was born and raised in Detroit, MI.
He is the author of the book *Brother Of Leaving*
(Marick Press) and the pamphlet *Heard Among The
Windbreak* (Eyewear Publishing). His writing has
appeared in many journals including *New Orleans Review*,
Passages North, *The Journal*, *Commonweal*, *Drunken Boat*
and *The Poetry Review*. He is a recipient of The Devine
Poetry Fellowship (judged by Terrance Hayes); he has
also been nominated for multiple Pushcart Prizes in both
poetry and creative nonfiction. He regularly reviews
collections of poetry for the radio program,
"Stateside," on Michigan Public Radio. He
currently lives in Dearborn, MI and teaches
at Oakland University.

TABLE OF CONTENTS

I

OUR FATHER, THE LOST GEOMETER

Down near the creek, Euclid Avenue floods
with brown-green water. I rest my right hand
on his *Elements* and swear that my life
will always be this circumscribed and small,
       a rite that goes by many names,
among them allegiance, temperament, weather.
My sister wanders out in a fog of obtuse angles.
She wears a Gore-Tex anorak to bear
the heavy rain that's falling from the north.
       Cataracts echo in the culvert;
the submersible pump emits its steady hum.
Last August I watched the mud of the creek bed
       dry to shaved ridges of bone
from the west-facing windows of my mother's house.
These drastic riparian shifts drown
and erase the stories nobody wants told.
I keep referring to Euclid as our father.
I keep guessing where the edges of this life
fall off into ensoulment. In bisecting
       the city he made us who we are,
a terminal series of squares and birthing lines,
as if this town were the geometry of grief
       and we were blameless.

AT THE PERIPATETIC SCHOOL OF RIVER ROUGE, MI

Take the dawn, take the drunkard's
afternoon and its cloying sunlight,
the '73 Camaro's gleaming pipes and fat
tires tearing up Great Lakes Boulevard
as evidence. For what is rising but anachrony,
and what earthly carapace can gleam
like this in a world of smoke? Your pockmarked face
repelled the others, so you scared up grouse
and listened to the questions
posed among the purple loosestrife beyond
the razor wire of the abandoned mill.
The killdeer atonally sings you away from
the delicate life it has hatched
in seams of rabble stone. Unlike you,
it only pretends to be wounded. There is a difference
between harbinger and talisman, between
departure and forgetting, intransigence
and the absence of a message.
Think of all the life that scurries
out of sight as you walk here at dusk,
the innumerable creatures that you have
almost glimpsed, our own species'
ability to hide in plain sight. The factory glows
ochre as the sun sets in its chipped-out windows;
it is a relic of a happier, more destructive time.
The wind sends coke from anthracite hills over
the river and cleaves the spores from
dandelion heads until Memorial Park teems
with grey and yellow. If we could identify
a common grief, it would bind us with its rhizomes

like sandy loam where Marram Grass
succeeds its own papery deaths and from us
perennial tubers and second-growth trees
would flower. See the translucent figure
with the cane emerging from the bulrushes?
How he also slides toward a future
that will pick out and disseminate the doomed?

GENUS EPHEMERA: FIGHT SONG OF THE FISH FLIES

In 1986 I saw a blimp land among glistening fish flies in an abandoned airfield on the western shore of Lake Erie near the Detroit River delta. The lake had recently rebounded from its eutrophic period of the mid-twentieth century, the blue-green algal blooms having dissipated as a result of EPA-mandated reductions of point-source pollution and with help, ironically, from the cyanobacteria-filtering capabilities of the invasive zebra mussel.

Like glass shattered over the tarmac, the flies crunched underfoot as we walked to meet the blimp captain (to clear them in healthy years takes brooms and shovels). He was unimpressive for a man of his station and Good Year allowed no passengers, which had us asking, "What's the point? To watch and aspire?" My cousin and I were never going to be blimp captain material, and we did not find the ponderous, non-rigid airship entertaining.

★

Each river is a sentence following its nouns polysyn-detonically down itself, thus to speak of rivers is to fall into tautology. Ellipses suggest the obvious destination of an inflated sentence while saving us the time. It will swift around the jetties, and even small rivers have big mouths that disgorge alluvial poison.

Roads follow their eponymous rivers and buckle at their bends. In Southeastern Michigan and Northeastern Ohio, rivers flood the lake with phosphorous during run-off from spring rain. Excess levels of phosphorous cause cyanobacteria, or "blue-green algae."

Our rivers of light pollute the night sky, which is why I cherish the Good Year shots wherein the night takes on a brilliance the human eye cannot afford it. I don't know that I've ever owned Good Years, but to merely connote positively in the consumer mind, regardless of purchase, is a victory in the company's long dirigible campaign.

★

The fish flies were very good signs for the overall health of the ecosystem, my uncle explained to us. That lifespan of two days during which they refuse to do anything but indiscriminately mate seems painfully short, though they are also afforded a season as nymphs in the sediment of the riverbed.

My spine is arched today like those gooey bellwethers from decades of sitting listlessly on couches watching sporting events, marveling at the accompanying shots of our sprawling city during nighttime telecasts, the miles of halogen lights tracing the path of water. I sometimes mute the television and listen to the hum of radial tires flowing south down Huron River Road and imagine roadside vistas that open up to lake views.

★

Today Erie is a bed of pseudofeces and daggering little shells. In recent years the toxic algal blooms began returning to the western basin. They were first captured by a blimp getting atmospheric coverage for a Cleveland Indians telecast. Two summers ago Toledo, Ohio's municipal water supply was contaminated by cyanobacteria. In cities like Toledo, 2014 was also a summer free of the putrid stench of fish flies, free of carcasses glommed onto sidewalks and awnings. Limnologists fear that by 2035…

TOLEDO

A Jeep Wrangler looms
above the pitted lot
of the closed-down Chrysler plant.

Toledo's emptiness is the one misnomer
that can bring the game birds back
to patchwork green spaces

sutured over post-industrial scars.
Toledo has towering blue spans
that cross the river

and a searing wind through trees
where the Maumee Bay
writhes in its torrent. Toledo

has gulls that cry like puppies
over produce tumbling
from the trucks at weekend market.

Toledo has a listless energy
that staggers through birdsong and hypodermic
needles in botanical gardens;

jackals, bamboo shoots
in the lairs of pandas at the zoo.
Storm doors with rusted handles

stuffed with health insurance offers,
handbills for pizza, epiphanic notes
blown out beneath a greening sky.

OFF-ROADING WITH PREVENIENT GRACE

This morning I pour a perfectly good fifth of Canadian whiskey down the sink, but I feel the lump of a pint bottle against my back as I slide onto the vinyl seat bench.

Old Blank Face rides beside me, pontificating in pallor-grey, solid as a wisp of nimbus. I fear him the way I fear that certain aphorisms are true.

God does not steer, nor does he buy any smokes, and if he did you would cease to believe.

Ethereal Job. Cryptic Wesley.

You cannot off-road in the spring. A Dodge Durango stuck in mud can be a metaphor for almost anything.

Engine squealing like a shoat in the brown field, wheels troughing into muck.

So unscrew the plate and chuck it in a culvert. The self is comprised of weather–ablated objects that nobody else can read.

He is on the hook to leave an extra set of footprints next to each allegorical pilgrim (so much of faith a trace of what we cannot see), two tire-prints in each parallel lane, two wings above each set of slumped and aching shoulders.

Grackles in ash limbs are the devil, the wind-turned leaves are greening nickels passed down out of pity, and nobody fears stale whiskey breath and beard if a man can sing.

I hop out of the truck and trudge toward the road.

The tree is deeper than the bug that sickens it, he calls after me.

I am hoping for a payphone where I can punch my father's number into cold steel squares, a little town where nobody knows anybody else, a town whose citizenry rests mute as pond-scum, a town where nothing's spoken out of earshot. I wander off, a stranger in my skin, seeing birds and discarded pop cans like signposts every mile or so.

DEARBORN

a hymn for Kevin Matthews, killed by an off-duty policeman
December 23rd, 2015

Our town is a sclerotic beast
whose sewer throats disgorge
the epithets of Orville Hubbard
and Henry Ford, where police
give chase beyond duty
or jurisdiction and kill
the unarmed suspects
of misdemeanor larceny.
It squeezes the slow
river guts to rapids.
Its nerves are shot;
it shakes the haws
and sugar maples
then drinks them under.
I love this place
as the tholepins creak
and we take turns rowing
down Shenandoah Street,
erstwhile floodplain.
Its makeshift cinderblock
levee spined through Spinks loam,
its concrete brow ringed
by a high-water mark
nobody thought this run-
off could surpass.
To love any city is violence.
The once-ambling body
snakes and hemorrhages;
thousands of muscles flicker

as it runs. Did I ever tell you
the story about the night
Henry Ford died?
The Rouge overran its banks;
his powerhouse flooded;
his brain bled into itself
like the outmoded machine
that it was, eagle-shaped
blood flecks congealed
in his hippocampus grooves
like posterity's dark prizes
as his corpse blued
and stiffened, no light
in his bedroom except
a candle and a wood fire.
I feel like I am always
telling you this story.
Do you also imagine
these blocks in leagues
of water, our bungalows
hurtling like failed arks
toward a new, unmapped sea,
until our brief existence
is a pseudo-history, a lesser
Atlantis nobody will search for?
We live and die in the riverain
which is the property
of everyone and no one.
It periodically lifts its haunches
from alluvium to chase us
off. But it makes sense
that we call our favorite places
haunts, given what we know
of geology and murder.

You were killed
behind Cardoni's Bar
the night that by virtue
of my skin I stood unbothered
on the banks and watched
the water rise,
trying to remind myself
that it was winter.

POINT PELEE

Tick of sleet on frozen sand, grey hours on the gunmetal shore of Erie,
geese knifing toward open water, breakwater pounding at the beach,

stone teeth licked by a thousand plosives, hoarse gulls lofting over spit.
In this bloody world what could be much worse nonetheless seems dire,

and when sorrow blows in one direction all afternoon across a numb
breadth of lake, the edge wave of pain is called a seiche.

My friend moved here after his divorce a few months back
to spend the winter in his parents' beach shack.

Though late March, it doesn't feel like spring.
We play Levon Helm songs on acoustic guitars near the woodstove.

Between "It Makes No Difference" and "The Night They Drove
          Old Dixie Down,"
he tells me the Canadian government wanted to force his parents

and their neighbors to sell to expand the national park,
but his dad hired some high-powered attorneys and managed to keep

the place in the family after he died.
My father called it his legacy, but I don't think he knew what "legacy" meant.

Still, he is glad to be here now where he can listen to the fire and water,
the littoral crinkling as it freezes beyond his deck.

In the evening we walk his dog through fields of abandoned tomato houses,
and he explains how Heinz left the town mostly unemployed two years ago.

When he dies he wouldn't mind if the property was ceded to the park.
Probably the best thing I could do.

We shiver as the dog romps and the wind whips
the ripped-up plastic sheets of the greenhouses.

Southern tip of Canada, lonely sand-spit,
odd place to be known for its tomatoes. Fine place to find the self

alone after decades as it silts from the homeland into the glacial lake.
We trail the dog back to the little cottage. The breakers now are brittle
      shelves of ice.

ON LEAVING ANCHORAGE

I have slept long years in the sunlight
and watched the sea ripple silver

in the pitch-black afternoon
until my cigarettes ran out.

It's geology that dwarfs us,

the thaw of epochs
that never quite begins,

the incommensurate scale of violated
body to silt coast to ocean,

the green and purple curtains
that hide the cold Cook Inlet.

It's this god-forsaken family

and its blighted history,
this genealogy that makes me

small. I close my eyes, a phosphene

becomes a woman in a red anorak
stuck in a mudflat as the tide rises

like spilled ink. I am not

the guilty one. I am a tiny organism
rasping the light season,

suckered to a stone in swale muck.

Here they do not prosecute the guilty.

MY FATHER'S NAMESAKES

I ask my father why
he named his cat Boccaccio.
An owl perches on a five-story

gantry crane, and Zug Island
belches holographic fire over
Southwest Detroit. He speaks of

interference and diffraction. My father
speaks of the river's black,
the black river like a bowling

ball with scratches of halogen,
moon, and starlight, and not
a river, he argues,

but a dredged-out creek
that pours into a river.
A willow's hair floats

atop the current. My father
says my bitterness is a hologram
without a reference beam.

I tell him it's a wonder
anyone Downriver speaks
given how much is only

partly answered, how little
is confessed, and how few
have the agency to hear

confessions. Boccaccio
scratches out a canto
on an impervious pane

of glass. My father reads
the interference pattern and
paws his snowy head.

I keep asking my father
if his cat Boccaccio is dead.
Even living cats have stone ears

that turn inward when they hunt.
I keep asking my father if his cat
Boccaccio will paw at the water

as it flows. *Refractions trouble deep*
blanks in the riverbed.
I ask my father

why he named me for his father.
Boccaccio made the canto
out of dust and wind,

but it's only an approximation
of our breaths. No one knows
what to measure or how;

a cat is its own prosodic lesson.
I ask my father
why he named me for his father.

It was an obvious name
for the scruffy little beast.
I ask my father why

he named me for his father.
Human it is to have compassion
on the unhappy, he finally says.

TUNGUSKA

The fourth thunder
was the thunder
most like thunder.

Nickel and light searing a
broken atmosphere. Bog craters,
millions of fallen trees.

After the first thunder
our clothes were hot.
I wanted to look

Nearly two decades later
Leonid Kulik found
silicate, magnetite,

at the trees
but their branches were on fire
and ash was falling in our eyes.

and nickel extra-terrestrial
in origin in bog peat
near the river.

I shielded my eyes
from the bright, vivid shapes.
The second thunder tossed us

hard. The strong wind
came. A sound like birds
flying overhead, like

Millions of fallen trees
and millions of others
stripped to blackened boles.

travelling birds. "Did you hear
the birds flying overhead?"
I asked my brother.

Yet *time flows*
because *no set*
of proofs

The ground at dusk
like a pustulance through gauze.
Nobody arrived for a very long time.

can be complete.
Holes exposing charred
root systems of trees.

I walked with Kulik
and saw this life
was very small and very large.

I'm told there were more pressing things
than studying this place—
a revolution, many wars to fight.

The meteor decohered
before
it ever struck.

In Europe
they reported
several vivid nights.

LONDON

What dumb thing were we living for last summer?
Horses clopping in Hyde Park,
goldcrest kinglets in the river birches,
a 23 in majuscule on the back of the young
Arabic boy walking before us with his mother.
Two weeks after Brexit, one day past
the Bastille Day Attack in Nice.
I was reading Philip Larkin's *The Whitsun Weddings*
on that trip, and you were reading a novel called
Spill, Simmer, Falter, Wither.
We wandered to the western bank and stood
on a bridge high above the turgid water of The Thames.
You snapped pictures of The Tower of London
and The Houses of Parliament.
We ducked into The National Gallery
as it started raining and stood inches from
Jan van Eyck's *The Arnolfini Portrait.*
To create an interference pattern
with a sight beam and mirrors makes
a second order mythology of the matrimonial life,
you said. *What we become in convexity*
belies the frailty of the little hands, clasped, though.
We made love in a little room in The Strand Palace Hotel
and listened afterwards to the West End Theater District
traffic, tourists en route to dinner
and quaint tragedies. We drank martinis
at The Savoy in a booth beneath a photograph
of Humphrey Bogart while an American
lounge pianist sang, *If you get lost between*
the moon and New York City, the best thing
you can do is fall in love, and I thought

of how even the stupidest song soothes
if put over at the right moment.
But what can the moon mean to the river
at neap tide? you whispered.
By what instrument beyond piano
does kairos transform the ephemeral?
The next morning we woke before dawn
and shuffled into a black taxi.
London is not feline and sallow at this hour,
as has been written. It doesn't tongue
the windows of cafes and taxi cabs.
I suddenly wondered what had been done
with all the rubble left over from the air raids
a half-century ago. Had it been shipped offshore
and disposed of in the depths of The North Sea?
Had it been repurposed for new buildings?
What is the imagination but a crude material,
like rebar, that bears all the extra weight?
I swear I heard you ask that last morning
on our way to Heathrow and Detroit.
Goodbye, I said, as our taxi
puttered up to the departure gates.

IN SEVEN ERSTWHILE CITIES

The dead have not been delivered
      their canes or walking shoes.

In two outfaced towers,
      two watchers see the pulses
of bipeds in infrared
      and see the lit ends of

      their cigarettes with naked eyes.

In three dozen empty houses,
      past scenes of trauma play
         upon the walls

as if those walls were screens.

      In Franco's Spain
the spirit of the dead keeps
         winning,

and it is clear to anyone
who listens

that the hillside stone
can speak.

In Laos, in the Plain
of Jars, some shattered
monuments persist

and the giants sleeping
deep within their lidless

     casements savor the lack

of footsteps and the gradual
                ensoulment
    of unexploded ordnance.

DOWNRIVER

That summer it got so I couldn't look at the horses in the pasture off Bredow Road without seeing myself engaged in every foul mammalian act a horse is prone to—the shitting, kicking, biting, slothfully chewing straw until the afternoon dwindles away, lying recumbent in the ammoniac stench of the sweating body.

"Each horse has its compulsions," Alana would say.

On the way back from her house in the country, or between pizza deliveries, I would stop to see Ben Egan at his father's bar where I'd drink cheap beer and study my sallow face in the backlit mirror. Collectible Budweiser steins, bobble heads, and Sambo dolls that Ben was always threatening to smash, just as he had been threatening to smash his father's skull since high school, sat on a shelf behind the bar. So far Walt's head remained full of Americana's ugly trinkets and Ben was still in the old man's employ.

~

"The organism is resilient," Alana said one evening, coming up after a line, while I wondered what our business was with mirrors and my dilated pupil dove into itself. She wanted to drink so we went where the drinks were next to free, but instead of Ben we found his bigot father who charged us full price or even a little more, we thought, and grumbled that his shiftless son had not shown up, Walt's shocks of curly white hair high-def in the mirror like the nape of a confederate general from a documentary we'd watched, and we began to suspect that we possessed certain hepatotoxic habits and properties we'd been denying and should stop blaming the nicotine-stained mirror for how we looked.

"The organism is made to self-regenerate," she said as we walked to my 1980 Buick in the gravel lot. "In this way it is unlike worn-out horses and old-ass cars."

~

Downriver everyone kept a casual pulse on the trains that ran from Ford Rouge to Woodhaven Stamping on down to Flatrock Mustang. Delivering pizzas for an outfit that gave them away for free after a half-hour wait, my interest went slightly beyond casual. Alana and I had waited many of these trains out, smoking cigarettes at crossings in my car, blaring bad rock 'n' roll and pretending to think. I have since disavowed all the half-concocted thoughts I had concerning time while watching trains pass except to remember how there were fewer and fewer of them that year. Either the place was dying or my timing was getting more impeccable.

~

That autumn Alana would head out west with a millwright she used to fuck; they'd both found work in the natural gas fields of Wyoming. That winter Ben would die of a heroin overdose. Walt tended to the dwindling clientele. I'd show up sometimes with my guitar and sing Rolling Stones songs he erroneously remembered his son having liked and think of how Alana taught me to cup my fingers beneath a horse's chin so it wouldn't bite me when I fed it carrots.

Though Walt insisted everything had changed, the afternoons still looked the same—sunlight in the dust motes of a quiet barroom, milkweed in the ditches and fields, monarchs floating through on their routes to Mexico, brood mares and geldings drowsing in their pastures, unlit railroad crossings with their arms raised.

II

ETUDE

For when the wind-turned leaves
of shoreline poplars tumble like coins
and the flesh becomes capillary
waves rippling down scales that don't

resolve and down those that only
the round gobies seem to hear,
having carried them from remote
salt waters in the ballast tanks of ships

singing, lest we had long ago forgotten,
Sand plunges toward the deep
where blind seas ride the spines
of animals from ancient epochs.

HEARD AMONG THE WINDBREAK

To bow with snow and mercury,
to stagger on shallow roots, to green
the needles on these arms and shed them,
to stand between the cold and you.
This is crop milk in a wren's throat
with no young to feed, grass blades
and garbage gummed with spit.
In the shadow of a derrick,
this is bitterness and home.
Strung with multi-colored flags,
spruces surround the backflow ditches
where the heron drink and sicken.
Skin the saffron color of the sand,
wrinkled like the paper sack
that holds the bottle, to be an old man rolling
Beech Nut over a blue tongue (the tongue,
that bellwether of splendor and disease),
listening to the branches sigh
and the meters on the jutting pipes tick,
spine curved like a taproot, smell of sick
river in the burdock whose root tincture
is said to cleanse us of abuse. When this was a park,
children with dirt-smudged faces
would watch from the trestle bridge
as carp fought over the popcorn
and breadcrumbs they sprinkled in brown water.
Now halogen light obscures dim
parabolas of stars whose names
I never knew, and razor wire glints.
To stand up while the chemicals roil
and the bedrock fractures,

to feel that and not fall, to be a soul
full of mourning doves and shudder
with startled wings as they rise.

ETUDE FOR A SONG

About the green skies I've refused
to drive beneath, green the color
of an empty bottle, about the muddy
culverts of Northeast Ohio sick
with phosphorous, about the car
I'd park athwart the ditch
and crawl beneath, about that
erroneous advice passed down
by my grandmother on what to do
if caught driving in a tornadic storm,
about the lupine bent to bare
their bracts, about the false
flowers of their multi-foliate
heads, about the ashes windblown
in riverain, about the rabble
stone wrapped in chain link
along the ditch's berm, about
the shadows of the convective
clouds like algal blooms
on the surface of Lake Erie,
about naming lakes and rivers
to connect them in our minds,
about the milk thistle and burdock
I have eaten, about these fictive
cures for our intractable abuses.

FIGHT SONG WITH TURTLE AND MALLARD

There is a black cough in the water.
There are no innocents.

Tadpoles swim in the shadows of ash limbs.

This is not the frog stuff of a fable,
though the face transforms and blurs

in the riffling capillaries
of the brown-green creek

and each moment is an instar
in the long deterioration of the body

(I read of how the turtle's liver
does not slow down with age).

This is princely nothing;

decades past the initial crimes, it is time

to appreciate the aesthetics of the damage:
the dead birch reaching toward us,

opalescent swirls on the surface
of the water. The mind elevates itself

like a pedestrian bridge
between the neighborhood and park.

We can count the stoneflies
and catalogue frog croaks

and marvel at the elegiac numbers.

It gets tempting to call what's left
resilience,

the mallard passing
beneath the bridge, the turtle

hunting snails along the sandy bottom.

FIGHT SONG TO BE SUNG BETWEEN THE TRADE WARS

An indeterminate animal lurches up ahead.

I live in this greening place of non-existent
tariffs where the heads of dandelions

explode and solidify over the course of a day,
their proliferation and geographical sprawl

making questions
of empathy and appropriation litigious.

I loved this town's manufacture
of common grief until I realized

its history was hyper-present,
its bigot fathers and belt-buckle-

beaten wantons, its cops chomping
pseudo-legalese in black faces.

We are sick of more than promises.
An untold cocktail of chemicals

rides the east air.
No one feels as though living once is adequate.

The smokestacks that tower over
obsidian hills blear the moonlight.

I turn and hoof it up the street
toward the slouching figure that might

hold a small death in its teeth
after all,

some sustenance embargoed long ago.

FIGHT SONG OF THE LAZAR HOUSE

Cindy has to chain the dog
to the banister
so it doesn't attack me,
some beagle mix,
purblind, fat.
She offers me
a cup of coffee as she lights
a cigarette in my grandmother's
kitchen and coughs
like a garbage disposal
with a loose blade.
She wears a shrunken
pink shirt,
faded pink with a yellow
nicotine limn, sweat
shorts and flip flops;
she has tallow skin, a goiter
like a waddle on her neck.
I found her an hour ago
at the strip mall
methodically searching
the potted plants and
sidewalk cracks for butts.
I took her to the Shell Station
and bought two packs
of Kools, figuring
this would keep her
home for the remainder
of the day.
This looks like my
grandmother's kitchen,

and it is my grandmother's
kitchen, but the doors
have been torn off
the cabinets and rows
of orange medicine bottles
sit where my grandmother's
teacups used to be.
When I ask Cindy
where my uncle has gone,
she says she doesn't
care and hopes
he never gets back,
that he backhands her
and calls her a whore,
patently untrue.
I sip the bitter instant
coffee and read
the labels on the bottles:
Lithium, Haliperodol,
Zoloft, Oxycontin;
not all of these scripts
are hers. She points
to a picture on the corkboard
above the telephone
and says it's me. No,
that's Uncle Thomas,
I correct her. No,
that's you, she insists.
I nod as I sit at the table
to wait. My grandmother
would sit in this chair
and chain-smoke
Doral cigarettes
while playing an interminable

game of solitaire.
The old man
stayed in his plush chair
in the den and
half-heartedly read
novels while watching
golf or baseball.
They are both gone now,
and I don't know
how my aunt
and my uncle
divide up the rooms
in this house.
I imagine there are
rooms
for dust-caked books
and rooms for
loose pennies, rooms
for pills that were
never taken and
rooms for empty
hangers, rooms for
errant memories, for
rumpled gowns
and collared shirts,
paternal rooms, maternal
rooms, carpeted rooms
for moieties in flux,
rooms of throw
pillows for a dog
to tear apart,
rooms for too many
pills ingested,
for hepatotoxic

bleeding out the eyes.
Cindy rolls
blue smoke over
her filmy tongue;
the idea to light
tobacco and inhale it
came from a dark,
contemplative
place, I think.
I give her a hug
before I leave.
Her dog growls
at the end of its
chain as I open
the door.

ETUDE FOR AN ELEGY

Your fingerpicks and capo
on the settee, a glass of water
and a small capsule
on a time release,

the burden of winter
in platelets and bones.
When I heard your dull
thud of chords last night

with the mouth harp melody
stringing itself through
"I Shall Be
 Released,"

I heard *chord, quark,* and *cork,*
strings oscillating
on a bridge of chiseled bone,
then thought of something

dead, like an empty bottle
or the tines in Tony's harp.
But who am I to define
a thing as dead?

All the good that can be done
is impossible, like this playing,
and help is the shape
that language whittles

out of failed intentions.
You told me words
are moody bastards
that have ceased

to love us, so I shut
my maudlin mouth.
A bracelet dangles
from your wrist,

traveling up your arm,
but the analogy to drugs
ends at the elbow.
I comb your matted hair

and curse the old guitar
that makes your fingers bleed
and fools us into thinking
time is stretching out.

THRENODY

for Bill McGettigan

Clear from the back of the place
I saw the blues player stomp
on death, through smoke
and diffuse yellow light,
his face: a fingerprint on a window.

~

I drove through a cataract of fog
this morning like a little
vein in sclera.

~

I saw consecutive funerals on a hangover
and two hours' sleep,
black limousines in rain, waiting
traffic. The last car
with its four flags is never slow enough.

~

A good funeral should stop the entire day.

A good day should trail its funeral
in rags.

TO BE SUNG AT CERTAIN FUNERALS

Black trusses of the drawbridge
gleam in river mist, that span

of iron work between Trenton and Grosse Ile.
My friend Brad Morris

drives his VW Rabbit forever
from the mainland to nowhere

listening to mix tapes and considering
the wild anachronies of heaven.

~

Radial tires of the procession
rumble over grates.

The Trenton Channel
rushes around the jetties

toward the big lake.

~

The family asked me to play guitar
and sing at the funeral. I hadn't spoken

to Brad in nearly ten years.
I felt like an impostor.

I wouldn't have wanted me there
if I were them. His father

was moved to tears,
explaining that I was a real friend

to Brad because I hadn't been
his friend during the bad times.

Some version of tough love,
some mess of grief and logic.

~

In the middle of the night,
in the floodlit shadow of a spire,
Brad pulls into a parking lot

and sees a deer's glowing eyes
in the shallow woods
behind the church. Votive candles

light the stain glass windows
of the atrium. He scrolls
the contacts in his phone,

looking for a high school
girlfriend's name, thinking he
has typed her in and she will

show up here, halated
like the dawn, to nurse him
from narcosis, that inveterate

track marks might sew themselves
of the needle's wake.

~

I picture him turning blue
after injection and the jaundiced woman
with the face tat and lip rings
shoving an ice cube
up him while dialing 911.

~

Each song is a vague guess
at its own meaning.

~

He is in in in
the many predicates
such as spirit, and night

predicated upon several
hours of naked daylight,
which leave us translucent

as gobies or saints,
finds all that inheres
and all that only seems

to disappear until somebody
breaks into sobs, or sings.

SONG

Of tourniquet and needle-
socket of the sore,
of turning and turning blue,
of the VW emblem
on the busted grill,
of the ice cube shoved up
the rectum in an attempt
to wake you from
your overdose, of failure,
of failure as the modicum.
Of dirt roads in Monroe, MI,
of tract houses
made of cinderblocks.
Of the peregrine face
I did not recognize
beneath the open lid.

FIGHT SONG OF THE PRONG-HORNED ANTELOPE

I am the thought of sage grass
in a horned skull, and more,

below the plexus, the splenic artery
thrums with bilge,

along the prairie highway
a silver tanker gleams

and the freight wind
dislodges ghost voices

with the banality of *whoosh,*
a sigh over deaths that cannot

truck from here. The backflow
ditches taste of silver, the water

like you could not imagine until
what films the blue tongue

pastes tongue to roof.
A fat woman pounds and huffs

as she collects dead grackles
for her freezer and performs

a daily autopsy; it should go
without saying no one

reads it. I do not
know the lexicon of chemicals.

I bleat and roam and swallow.

FIGHT SONG OF THE ROACHES

The fipronil has left us drunk.
Paper spines, frayed spines,
names of worlds on spines,
we slumber like readers
in their abandoned books.
We burrow into each other
while masticating text
(carcass and damp pulp,
the sour smell of breath)
and laying ourselves down in majuscule.
We've staggered too,
seen the undersides of leaves
in canary-yellow, scarlet,
and grocery-store-bag brown
as we drank of them.
Some of us hiss through spiracles
and die, others sleep
in the chipped-out mortar
between the bricks.
The sun captures the best
and worst alike in various stages
of slouching ambulation, God,
as we slow and sicken.

FIGHT SONG OF THE FIDDLEBACK

The rain tonight
dribbled through the silver
maple leaves long
after it had rained.

I sang a few bars
of Guy Clark's "Dublin
Blues," thinking of the spider
I hit with a boot
this afternoon for nothing
but fear and all
the pests I am always
killing to assuage
its grip. Yesterday

my wife couldn't tell
whether roaches
or crickets scattered
when she moved
the planter in the yard.
Crickets, luckily,
she realized when
one hopped.

Harbingers of August,
and we don't mind
having their songs in
our heads.

Spiders of the sort
(brown recluse?) I found

this afternoon hunt
roaches and other
insects we do not want
around. I worry over

what potting soil
and damp cardboard
will bring into the garage.
I am the type
to stay up all night
with vague foretellings
of reckonings
as I imagine
the collapsed spider
carcass
extending its legs
once again
and scurrying away
in a gesture of weary
forgiveness though
there is nothing
a spider or a person
has the agency
to forgive. I haven't

had a drink in 24 hours.
I am as clean as this
little house, organs
as mulched, likely,
as its worst beams.

FIGHT SONG TO BE SUNG AT COUNTY FAIRS

You turned around once or twice,
but I was not there.
All songs begin this way,
with a memory or figment.
We were no longer of that place,
but we were not on our way either.
I miss you, too, and I'm sorry
the leaves seem to be limned
in this particular hue of light
(I think it's halogen or moon).
My first impulse
was to look westward down
the road toward my childhood,
transparent but enigmatic enough
to not be a childhood at all.
We never know what sets us off,
and nothing can stop us but decorum.
Given all that we have shared,
wouldn't it be best to go nowhere?

FIGHT SONG OF THE POPLARS

Bruised with blades at the bight
and bleeding in the gums of saws,
felled poplars in the riverain
in summer. Thick leaves coated

in sawdust like tongues
of thirsty ruminants, like chalky
tongues after a night of drink
and smoke. Ponderous, turgid

water, of all that might be said,
I'll listen to a furrowed
grey one in a southwest wind
on a bright foreboding day in June.

FIGHT SONG OF THE BROKEN SHOVEL

In a world of white, my spine
is too sick to register the snow.

The hard ground still
administers its ache.

The snow fleas work interminably unseen,
saying, "Death is one function;
do not call it 'rest.'"

I do not call it.
Nobody mentions it up here.

In a world of shovels,
I am the gripless one

amidst their throaty machines
boisterous as drunks,
too tired to wish anybody well.

Hoarse with scraping,
and the injury gets worse
on days like this;

I am past the point
of healing with rest.

As creatures go, we
are unregenerate.

FIGHT SONG OF THE LIMPET

I've mistimed the sea again,
suckered to a wet stone
at low tide, radula rasping

algae from its face,
stemmed eyes pointed
up at the barking gulls.

I slip beneath the mantle.
I hold and wait for
the stupid moon to tilt.

FIGHT SONG OF THE LITTLE HORSE

For meadows of yawning
and imagining set aside a fund.

There is no point anymore
in putting shoulders to the plow.

A girl sits on a hay rake
in a blear of sunlight,

a lume of moonlight rises
above the eye line of the field

at dusk, ears of hard corn
lie spilled in the mud.

Listen for the wind's forage
among the dying stalks,

the faint, percussive music
as the eohippus starts to gallop

over this fallow ground again.

INVECTIVE AGAINST MOURNING DOVES

They coo in the spruce behind Stu Price's house, trying to soothe me
with their nonsense. I sit in my dead friend's living room listening
to a Bix Beiderbecke 78. His children are huddled in the kitchen
describing a man I did not know to neighbors who did not visit
the old violinist or care much for the strange music that he played.
They stay in their roosts long past dawn on the frigid days.
They were once called Carolina Pigeons.
That trumpet tone does not sound like a dove; pigeon is no clarion.
Stu did not screech or moan though there must have been great pain
given what was in his bones.
Their wings screech as they take off to fly,
So sorry for your loss,
wired to return to wherever they feel safest and to panic
at the rustle of last year's leaves.

III

EPISTLE TO THE COPS ON A WINTRY NIGHT

Dear historical ambling
in a souped-up Ford, dear steel
gaze hidden behind tinted glass,
keeping these hours, everything
is a question of before
or after dawn. Your briefs spell out
blank descriptions of men
whose retreating shadows have been glimpsed
at the scenes of nearly-executed crimes;
not red-eyed and wandering,
but black male on foot, possibly armed,
suspicious. Before dawn,
those hours between bar
and liquor store when the nerves pull taut
and the birds start with their racket,
hours no do-gooder is awake to bless,
when the dreams of the civic mind
grow skittish with wild imaginings.
Post-dawn but not quite day and not
fully-decomposed on the garage floor,
I find the bones of poisoned mice:
of this, I am among the guilty.
"I held a mouse skeleton to my eye
like a monocle while snow
kept blanketing the warren that slopes
toward the frozen river
in shades not exactly white
and subnivean snow fleas
and vagrants eluded your shrill light"
is a sort of alibi.

The habits of this body
are not illegal; the real thefts
were not committed in the streets.
My boot prints in the white
are not illegal. You can follow
their tracks from creek to storefront
until the next squall buries them.

EPISTLE TO A THANE

Dear loose-twined leaves of sweet clover and chaff,
heart like a vole in the thresher, dear myriad
deductions for tardiness and un-mowed stubble,
austere son of a cunt counting silver to a Beethoven
scroll in the mechanical piano, who will feed us
when what we're owed is less than what we owe?
Dear demesne sprawled beyond your purblind sights,
dear phallus palmed in some interior red-curtained room,
out here the wheat shimmers like a sea
and gold is the color of pangs along
the stomach lining and the lining of the spleen.
Dear Phaethon yoked to noble generations,
dear patrilineal blessing, virtue powdered
clean of its mammalian scent, dear pitchfork-weary
patron of just rewards, we hear you are in the market
for a walking horse. Dear patrolling myopic eye,
gas-lit gravel walk, procurer of plow-mules
and grist for pone, I keep chewing straw and tasting sweat.

EPISTLE TO A LAZAR

Dear cigarette butts
in a dime purse and no words
to curse a traffic light,
dear war of nicotine and Haldol

in a gnashing mind,
dear stuffing shocked
from the right sleeve
of a coffee-splotched coat,

nails scratching sores
to pustulance, your body
is an outmoded machine
that channels prophecies

no one else hears
in your generation's most ridiculous
rock 'n' roll. You try to feed
the Internet jukebox coins

but cannot find the slot.
Your SNAP card will not buy
the Billy Joel song
stuck in your head.

Dear earworm, dear yellow
broodmare's teeth, dear crashing
party, dear fricatives
spat like hot oil, this Monday

they will pick you up again,
though they will not understand
and there will be many questions
about what to do with you.

EPISTLE TO A TABELLARIUS

Dear slaving long roads
    hour of ink on ephemeral pulp
accordion shut the leaf bark

when you set out
    dear ligatures in wax shielded
from the eyes of the republic

dear palimpsestic greeting
    SPD dear evanescent
 glyph

dear ampersand hashtag
    pound and pounding feet
on adverbial stone

dear colony of tongues
    wagging like broken
saddle straps dear

abbreviating virus
    our words hover
over you like whispers

transmissions of wars
    we execute
        but never fight

EPISTLE TO THE INNOCENT

But it is not permissible that the authors of devastation should also be innocent.
It is the innocence which constitutes the crime.

— James Baldwin

Dear happy tenant, as the yellow house across the road
recedes into the night, their killing outpaces your intentions.
Dear Joy, Elation, Mirth, your dog carries a shadow in its teeth,
and your euphemisms do not recuse you. This light isn't peculiar.
At no hour can the light be called "peculiar," though we have
peculiar words for light: "crepuscular," "prismatic," "refulgent."
Your shadow stands before them like a square mouth.
A throat clears, a sensor light goes off, radiating a blank
in your sight. Grace is the shape of light that isn't cast,
a cloak the dead will never wear, so stop moving your feet, stop
localizing sin, especially in the hands. You can only reach
for what is in your reach. Your figure elongates into obscenity as you call
the animal back, ignoring its news about the dark. Go forth:
enumerate the bodies. Count your habits before the glowing wreath.

EPISTLE TO A SCULLERY BOY

Dear face in the dormer grey as a gibbous moon,
dear leaning sleep in the dim mahogany hall,
dear yanked from your narcosis by the hair,
dear fly on the wall, stone tongue
enstoned to stone these 16 hours,
dear hiss of gargoyles pissing rain from rooftops,
green runnels of a green night, dear fingers
pruned in suds, high-water mark of wrists,
slop of chamber pots and stumbling gait,
dear timorous quaver in the voice, their cast-off
heirlooms shine behind your eyes.

EPISTLE TO AN ALEWIFE

Dear froth skimmed from the mug like dust,
dear fiddle-strap hung from carpenter's nail
and tenor voice, dear blue jukebox light,
dear obsolete noun pregnant with debunked expectations,
after you the dolts have immemorially hungered.
Dear typewriter clack in 6/8 time, I keep
writing letters in the worn-out lexicon of bigots.
Dear footsteps on grouted stone, dear catcalls in the head,
I bought you a lily from the old Hispanic woman
who sells them bar to bar from a dirty painter's bucket.
Dear iron chandelier in crepuscular light,
dear empty amber bottle and disembodied aches,
I will shake loose a cigarette for you and burn
this white moth that vectors toward tomorrow.

EPISTLE TO A COSTERMONGER

Dear bony fingers knotted like an apple bough,
I am walking out of time again, chewing
Red Delicious skin and listening to ruminant
guts hunger after meat. Braying voice, matter,
voice, ventriloquy of storefront and pavement,
I am like this fish with bone tassels woven
through its meat, and you are like a horse
with little meat on its life or like the clop
of that horse's hooves as it trudges through
an evanescent town with the orchard keeper's dray.
We exchange bright coins like wind-turned leaves
in the afternoon sun. This stench, this
interminable song that brings us to your stall.
Even in your obsolescence, I hear you everywhere.

EPISTLE TO A CHANGELING

Dear bright-eyed wanton
the body is preposterous and sad
we lift ourselves from porcelain
after the same retching our mothers
once mistook for love
tomorrow the cavalcade reverts
to the tableau it was before I spoke
before I saw you born
like a trickle in a dry creek bed
nobody parades here unless
there is a victory or death
and their horses high-step
anachronistically into the teeth
of traffic it's a miracle life
gets done at all and it's no crime
that it is ugly as all of us I remember
a season you got so tired of common birds
singing you awake just as you
were lying down that blue season
between autumn and winter I startled
a family of mallards from
their roost as I read the so-called
obscenities you scrawled in aerosol paint
beneath the railroad bridge

EPISTLE TO THE BANDOG

Dear pissing in the milkweed in the gravel,
hoarse after gnashing blades of grass,
green spittle on patio stone, acid in the throat,
I write to you as you bark dust from our age-old complaint:
I wish I knew where I belonged
and what my task was and where it ended.
I wish fences meant what they mean
to you. I am the grey image in a canine skull,
the one relieved that you are on a chain.
I'm told the pinion of your jaw locks up when you tear into flesh.
My boot-soles scrape; nobody lets me shout.
Dear guttural and plosive, the property that you guard
in vain (the bicycles, prescriptions, and mowers,
the electronics that amorphous shadows come for)
has already been stolen, and this imperative
to beware is almost comical. Dear twitching nose,
I am the smell of ammonia, dirt, and sweat.
I would growl in my direction too
if I had your booming voice.

EPISTLE TO A MALT-WORM

Dear rasp around the edges of the voice,
dear atonal rendition of a Gordon Lightfoot song,
dear weevil in the dry husk of my ear
cursing the governor, masticating
his kangaroo congress, those plutocratic
sycophants, for robbing working people of their rights.
Dear red-eyed dipsomaniac, the stench
of cheap whiskey doesn't make you wrong.
Dear dead before 60, dear fatal resignation,
dear nothing's dear or true beyond
the rigid shape of history and death,
dear plethora of classist nouns for you,
nobody cares that the Edmund Fitzgerald
was on its way to Great Lakes Steel on Zug Island
when it sank, though you say it like a source of pride,
you say it like a doomed and storied ship.
Because you work amid refineries and coke
in a neighborhood where people scrub
their awnings with toilet bowl cleanser
to remove the untold sludge and falcons perch
on giant gantry cranes to hunt, because your greens
are splotched with chemical stains like misshapen
homunculi, they simply hear
the slurred braying of a dying animal
as they throw you out.

EPISTLE TO AN ATHENIAN

Dear Theseus, were you able
to follow the string drawn
out like a chalk line,

or did we feed you to the beast?
Dear thick neck,
dear loose cigarettes,

were you able to rustle up
that money for the bus?
Did I say chalk line?

I meant chalk outline,
I meant cold, amorphous
trace of an erstwhile life.

Didn't I see you on Telegraph
Road last winter, your creaking
bicycle angled into the wind,

posing impossible questions
to the sloshing grey?
Didn't I see your strangulation

by municipal authorities
in a town so archetypal
it could be any town?

Does it matter what I have seen?
Each ephemeral city faces
fire or deluge before becoming myth;

they all disappear beneath
the polished weight
of their names—*Atlantis, Carthage,*

Detroit—and the helmets clash.
I refuse to give the evidence
you haven't asked for because

you and I both know
the shape of things:
Euclidian and brutal,

a hexagonal series folding
in upon its rotten beams.
Dear dark in a dark hour,

dear quiet, empty,
full of fear, there is slush
beneath our tires.

The spokes' web turns
me like a sail.
I never saw you nowhere,

but I guess at you
while legalese accounts
for all the dead and snow

breeds our senescence.
In my own head or looking
out the window,

given history or its absence,
I pause from the day's
occupations to tag your battered

toe like a new calf's ear.

EPISTLE TO A DRAY HORSE

Dear canting hat rack of an animal,
dear fuchsia sore beneath a twisted

girth strap, dear froth on martingale,
flayed whip marks on dun buttocks,

dear clopping in the head, green
spittle on the snaffle bit, dear aching

spine and barking fetlock, the men
with boutonnieres pinned to their coats

have us yoked to time, pocket
watches ticking at their breasts

like flies against the coach.

EPISTLE TO THE EDGE OF TOWN

Dear slouching ghost among
        the purple loosestrife
where the steel mill used to stand,

people tell me stories about you,
        and I believe them.

They say you are scarecrow thin,
        arms pustuled and scabbed.
Dear Veterans Park

where homeless sprawl
with donut boxes full of

change and toothpick flags,
        dear tinny Springsteen number
on a factory-installed

car stereo, asthmatic cough
        in the partial

dark, this river is no border
        and the riparian
has no edge. Dear staggering late

into bars where no one
wants you and shouting for a taste,
        dear gaunt resurrection,

I used to think the killdeer
with the crooked wing
       screeching

among the rabble stone
was only pretending
       to be wounded.

POSTSCRIPT TO THE EQUINE LETTERS

Dear brute insistence trudging the littoral
that the breakwater silts and scrambles
with its foam. Dear foaming estuary
neck like the flecked black leather of
a breastplate, this body, with its grotesque
absurdities, wears me out, belching
up acid, braying other peoples' songs,
coveting the freedom of water, pissing
into the dark as gulls cry and a sad song
plays on a little telephone in my breast
pocket. Ears pinned back, bickering,
I have praised the equine qualities of waves;
I have praised the intolerance of gulls
riding waves and watched stones sludge
toward the shelf's decline into green depths.
I was an equestrian riding all of it for a time,
but I am done writing letters to different kinds
of horses determined not according to breed
but economic purpose, epistle to dray,
jade, and cutting horse, sinking
my negligible weight into the spine
of a blinded animal, the poison
in its spleen propelling it forward,
not my heels, not the crop
of wind thwacking at its flank, into
the obsolescence it no longer
has the heart to fear.

NOTES

The final italicized lines in "My Father's Namesakes" are borrowed from Boccaccio's *Decameron*.

The italicized lines in "Tunguska" come from Rae Armentrout's poem, "Relations."

All spelling and grammar, as well as punctuation, follows American usage at the request of the author.

ACKNOWLEDGEMENTS

I'd like to thank the editors of the following journals for first publishing these poems:

Baltimore Review: "Our Father, The Lost Geometer" and "To Be Sung At Certain Funerals"
Bareknuckle Poet: "Fight Song Of The Fiddleback," "Fight Song of the Lazar House," and "Epistle To A Malt-Worm"
Canary: "In Seven Erstwhile Cities" and "Heard Among The Windbreak"
Cleaver Magazine: "Epistle To The Cops On A Wintry Night"
The Cossack Review: "Epistle To A Scullery Boy"
Cruel Garters: "Toledo"
Emerge Literary Journal: "Epistle To The Edge Of Town"
Fjords Review: "Epistle To An Alewife" and "Epistle To A Beldam"
Ghost Town Lit Mag: "Epistle To A Tabellarius"
Hamilton Stone Review: "Epistle To A Lazar," "Epistle To A Thane," "On Leaving Anchorage," and "Fight Song With Turtle And Mallard"
The Hobart: "Downriver"
The Lake Contemporary Poetry Webzine: "Song"
Literary Orphans: "Epistle To A Changeling"
London Grip: "Invective Against Mourning Doves"
Masque And Spectacle: "Epistle To Abraham Zapruder"
The McNeese Review: "Off-Roading With Prevenient Grace"
The Moth: "Epistle To A Dray Horse"
New Orleans Review: "Epistle To A Costermonger"
One: "At The Peripatetic School Of River Rouge, MI"

Old Northwest Review: "Point Pelee"
The Poetry Review: "Dearborn"
Posit: "Epistle To The Innocent" and "My Father's Namesakes"
RHINO: "Fight Song Of The Little Horse"
Slipstream: "Fight Song Of The Roaches"
Southword: "Etude For An Elegy"
The Sycamore Review: "Epistle To A Bandog"
Tirage Monthly: *The Journal Of Applied Poetics*: "Fight Song To Be Sung At County Fairs"
Wisconsin Review: "Threnody"

I'd also like to thank the following individuals: Todd Swift, Edwin Smet, Alex Payne, and the wonderful team at Eyewear Publishing. Mariela Griffor, F. Daniel Rzicznek, Larissa Szporluk, Abigail Cloud, Marshall Kitchens, Ryan Dillaha, Ann Delisi, Steve Cousins, Lori Ostergaard, Jim Nugent, Claire Crabtree, Nicholas Rombes, Michael Barry, Matt Balcer, Amanda Laudig, David Hammontree, Robert Keast, Patrick O'Neill, Brian Jabas Smith, Maggie Harstad, Roxanne Lapuma, Emily Freeman, Joe Linstroth, Mercedes Mejia, Larry Larson, Glen Armstrong, Kelly Fordon, Alise Alousi, Matt Burkett, Karen Brehmer, and Michael Lauchlan. Special thanks to Sarah Pazur, my everything, for her guidance and support.

⟁ EYEWEAR PUBLISHING

EYEWEAR'S TITLES INCLUDE

EYEWEAR
POETRY

ELSPETH SMITH DANGEROUS CAKES
CALEB KLACES BOTTLED AIR
GEORGE ELLIOTT CLARKE ILLICIT SONNETS
HANS VAN DE WAARSENBURG THE PAST IS NEVER DEAD
BARBARA MARSH TO THE BONEYARD
DON SHARE UNION
SHEILA HILLIER HOTEL MOONMILK
MARION MCCREADY TREE LANGUAGE
SJ FOWLER THE ROTTWEILER'S GUIDE TO THE DOG OWNER
AGNIESZKA STUDZINSKA WHAT THINGS ARE
JEMMA BORG THE ILLUMINATED WORLD
KEIRAN GODDARD FOR THE CHORUS
COLETTE SENSIER SKINLESS
ANDREW SHIELDS THOMAS HARDY LISTENS TO LOUIS ARMSTRONG
JAN OWEN THE OFFHAND ANGEL
A.K. BLAKEMORE HUMBERT SUMMER
SEAN SINGER HONEY & SMOKE
HESTER KNIBBE HUNGERPOTS
MEL PRYOR SMALL NUCLEAR FAMILY
ELSPETH SMITH KEEPING BUSY
TONY CHAN FOUR POINTS FOURTEEN LINES
MARIA APICHELLA PSALMODY
TERESE SVOBODA PROFESSOR HARRIMAN'S STEAM AIR-SHIP
ALICE ANDERSON THE WATERMARK
BEN PARKER THE AMAZING LOST MAN
ISABEL ROGERS DON'T ASK
REBECCA GAYLE HOWELL AMERICAN PURGATORY
MARION MCCREADY MADAME ECOSSE
MARIELA GRIFFOR DECLASSIFIED
MARK YAKICH THE DANGEROUS BOOK OF POETRY FOR PLANES
HASSAN MELEHY A MODEST APOCALYPSE
KATE NOAKES PARIS, STAGE LEFT
JASON LEE BURNING BOX
U.S. DHUGA THE SIGHT OF A GOOSE GOING BAREFOOT
TERENCE TILLER THE COLLECTED POEMS
MATTHEW STEWART THE KNIVES OF VILLALEJO
PAUL MULDOON SADIE AND THE SADISTS
JENNA CLAKE FORTUNE COOKIE
TARA SKURTU THE AMOEBA GAME
MANDY KAHN GLENN GOULD'S CHAIR
CAL FREEMAN FIGHT SONGS
TIM DOOLEY WEEMOED
MATTHEW PAUL THE EVENING ENTERTAINMENT